HOPE, HEALING AND RISING STRONG

THE POWER OF FORGIVENESS

OVERCOMING EMOTIONAL ABUSE

M L Ruscsak

The Power of Forgiveness: Overcoming Emotional Abuse

Trient Press
3375 S Rainbow Blvd
#81710, SMB 13135
Las Vegas,NV 89180

Ordering Information:
Quantity sales. Special discounts are available on quantity purchases by corporations, associations, and others. For details, contact the publisher at the address above.
Orders by U.S. trade bookstores and wholesalers. Please contact Trient Press: Tel: (775) 996-3844; or visit www.trientpress.com.

Printed in the United States of America

Publisher's Cataloging-in-Publication data
Ruscsak, M.L.
A title of a book :The Power of Forgiveness: Overcoming Emotional Abuse
ISBN
Paperback   978-1-955198-02-8
E-book   978-1-955198-01-1

CHAPTER 1: INTRODUCTION

- ❖ Explanation of emotional abuse and its effects
- ❖ Personal experience with emotional abuse and journey towards forgiveness
- ❖ Importance of forgiveness in healing from emotional abuse

Emotional abuse is a devastating and often overlooked form of trauma that can have lasting effects on a person's well-being. It can leave survivors feeling alone, unworthy, and deeply wounded. For many, the journey to healing and forgiveness can be long and arduous.

In this book, we will explore the power of forgiveness as a tool for overcoming emotional abuse. Drawing from personal experience and the stories of other survivors, we will delve into the complexities of emotional abuse and its effects on our lives. We will examine the challenges of forgiving those who have hurt us, and explore the rewards that come with releasing the burden of anger and resentment.

My own journey towards forgiveness has been a winding road, marked by moments of pain, confusion, and ultimately, transformation. It has been a process of unlearning old beliefs, letting go of toxic patterns, and embracing a new way of being. Through my own experience, I have come to understand the importance of forgiveness in the healing process, and I hope to share that with you.

This book is for anyone who has experienced emotional abuse and seeks a path towards healing and forgiveness. Through survivor stories, practical exercises, and uplifting quotes, we will explore the power of forgiveness to transform our lives and rise strong from our struggles.

Explanation of emotional abuse and its effects

Emotional abuse is a type of abuse that can have profound effects on a person's mental and emotional well-being. It is a pattern of behavior that is designed to control, manipulate, and undermine another person's sense of self-worth and autonomy. Emotional abuse can occur in any relationship, including romantic partnerships, familial relationships, and even in the workplace.

In this chapter, we will explore the definition of emotional abuse, the various types of emotional abuse, and the effects it can have on a person's life.

Definition of Emotional Abuse

Emotional abuse is a form of abuse that involves the use of emotional manipulation, intimidation, or control to diminish another person's sense of self-worth and autonomy. It is characterized by a persistent pattern of behavior that is intended to cause emotional harm.

Emotional abuse can take many forms, including verbal abuse, psychological abuse, and emotional neglect. It can involve a wide range of behaviors, such as belittling, criticizing, gaslighting, controlling, and isolating the victim.

Types of Emotional Abuse

Verbal Abuse: This type of emotional abuse involves the use of words to demean, criticize, or intimidate another person. It can include name-calling, insults, yelling, and constant criticism. Verbal abuse can be extremely damaging to a person's self-esteem and can lead to feelings of shame, guilt, and worthlessness.

Psychological Abuse: This type of emotional abuse involves the use of tactics such as gaslighting, manipulation, and mind games to control and manipulate another person. It can involve making the victim doubt their own perceptions, memory, and sanity. Psychological abuse can be particularly insidious, as it can be difficult to detect and may leave the victim feeling confused, helpless, and powerless.

Emotional Neglect: This type of emotional abuse involves the failure to provide emotional support, validation, and attention to another person. It can involve ignoring the victim's emotional needs, dismissing their feelings, and failing to provide them with the support they need to thrive. Emotional neglect can be especially damaging in childhood, as it can lead to developmental issues and attachment difficulties.

Effects of Emotional Abuse

The effects of emotional abuse can be long-lasting and far-reaching. Emotional abuse can impact a person's sense of self-worth, their ability to trust others, and their ability to form healthy relationships. It can also have physical effects, such as chronic stress, sleep disturbances, and digestive issues.

Here are some of the most common effects of emotional abuse:

Low self-esteem: Emotional abuse can cause a person to doubt their own worth and value. They may believe that they are unworthy of love and respect, and that they deserve to be treated poorly. This can lead to a cycle of self-doubt and negative self-talk that can be difficult to break.

Anxiety and depression: Emotional abuse can cause chronic stress and anxiety, which can lead to depression and other mental health issues. Victims of emotional abuse may experience symptoms such as panic attacks, difficulty sleeping, and feelings of hopelessness.

Trust issues: Emotional abuse can erode a person's ability to trust others. They may become suspicious or fearful of others' intentions, and may struggle to form healthy relationships.

Attachment issues: Emotional abuse in childhood can lead to attachment difficulties later in life. Children who experience emotional neglect may struggle to form healthy attachments with others, which can impact their ability to form healthy relationships as adults.

Difficulty regulating emotions: Emotional abuse can make it difficult for a person to regulate their emotions. They may experience intense feelings of anger, sadness, or anxiety, and may struggle to manage these emotions in healthy ways.

Isolation and loneliness: Emotional abuse can cause a person to feel isolated and lonely, as they may feel unable to connect with others or may have been intentionally isolated by their abuser. This can lead to feelings of social isolation and a lack of support, which can exacerbate the effects of emotional abuse.

Physical symptoms: Emotional abuse can have physical effects on the body, such as chronic stress, headaches, digestive issues, and other physical symptoms. These physical symptoms can compound the emotional toll of the abuse and make it more difficult to recover.

The effects of emotional abuse can be especially damaging in childhood, as they can impact a person's development and self-esteem. Children who experience emotional abuse may struggle with academic performance, social relationships, and mental health issues later in life.

It is important to note that the effects of emotional abuse are not limited to the victim alone. Emotional abuse can have a ripple effect on the victim's relationships with others, their ability to parent effectively, and their ability to contribute to society.

Conclusion

Emotional abuse is a devastating form of abuse that can have profound effects on a person's mental and emotional well-being. It is characterized by a persistent pattern of behavior that is intended to control, manipulate, and undermine another person's sense of self-worth and autonomy.

Emotional abuse can take many forms, including verbal abuse, psychological abuse, and emotional neglect. It can impact a person's self-esteem, their ability to trust others, and their ability to form healthy relationships. Emotional abuse can also have physical effects on the body, such as chronic stress and other physical symptoms.

In the next chapter, we will explore the journey towards healing and forgiveness after emotional abuse. We will examine the challenges of forgiving those who have hurt us, and explore the rewards that come with releasing the burden of anger and resentment. Through survivor stories, practical exercises, and uplifting quotes, we will explore the power of forgiveness to transform our lives and rise strong from our struggles.

Personal experience with emotional abuse and journey towards forgiveness

Have you ever felt like no matter what you do, you just can't do anything right? Or no matter how hard you try, someone in your life is always screaming at you? I have. My journey with emotional abuse began at a young age, and it lasted for many years. It wasn't until I began to understand the impact of emotional abuse on my life that I was able to break free and start the journey towards healing and forgiveness.

Growing up, emotional abuse was a constant in my life. It came in many forms, from verbal abuse and psychological abuse to emotional neglect. I never felt good enough, no matter how hard I tried. My abuser would constantly tear me down, criticize my every move, and make me feel small and insignificant. The emotional abuse was intertwined with physical abuse, which made it even harder to escape.

One of the most common threads in my experience with emotional abuse was disconnection. I felt disconnected from the world around me, and I struggled to form healthy relationships with others. My abuser isolated me from my friends and family, and I felt completely alone. I would try to please my abuser, to make them happy, but nothing I did was ever good enough. The emotional abuse was like a weight that I carried with me every day, dragging me down and making me feel worthless.

Despite all of this, there were moments of kindness and tenderness. My abuser would hug me and tell me they loved me, only to tear me down again moments later. There were empty promises to control their outbursts, only to have the next day be worse than the last. It was a never-ending cycle of abuse, and I felt trapped.

It wasn't until I started to identify the common threads in my experience with emotional abuse that I began to see a way out. I read books and sought out mentors who could help me understand the impact of emotional abuse on my life. I learned about the signs of emotional abuse, and I started to see the patterns in my own experience.

As I began to understand the impact of emotional abuse on my life, I started to see that there was a way out. I began to take small steps towards breaking free from my abuser, and I started to seek out help and support from others. It was a long and difficult journey, but with the help of others, I was able to break free.

The journey towards healing and forgiveness has been a long one. Learning to trust again when every instinct is telling you not to is difficult. It requires vulnerability and openness, which can be scary when you have been hurt before. But as I started to open up and share my story with others, I began to see the power of forgiveness and healing.

Forgiveness is not about forgetting what has happened or excusing the behavior of the abuser. It is about releasing the burden of anger and resentment, and finding a way to move forward. It is about taking back control of your life, and refusing to let the abuse define you.

Through my journey towards forgiveness, I have learned that it is possible to rise strong from even the most difficult of experiences. It takes courage and determination, but it is possible. I have found strength in survivor stories, practical exercises, and uplifting quotes. I have learned to see the power of forgiveness to transform our lives and rise strong from our struggles.

In conclusion, emotional abuse can have a profound impact on a person's life, but it is possible to break free and start the journey towards healing and forgiveness. Identifying the common threads in your experience with emotional abuse can help you understand the impact it has had on your life, and seek out the help and support you need to break free. Forgiveness is a powerful tool that can help in the healing process, but it is not a quick or easy fix. It requires a lot of introspection and reflection on one's own emotions and experiences.

One important thing to remember is that forgiveness does not mean forgetting or excusing the behavior of the abuser. It is important to hold them accountable for their actions and take steps to ensure your own safety and well-being. Forgiveness is not for their benefit, but for your own. It allows you to release the anger and resentment you may be holding onto, and move forward with your life.

In my own journey towards forgiveness, I found that it was a process that took time and a lot of work. I had to learn to be kind and patient with myself, and to acknowledge that healing is not linear. There were times when I thought I had made progress, only to find myself triggered by a certain situation or memory and feeling like I was back at square one. But through therapy, self-reflection, and a lot of support from loved ones, I was able to make progress towards forgiving my abuser and letting go of the pain and anger I had been holding onto for so long.

Ultimately, my journey towards forgiveness was a journey towards self-love and self-acceptance. It was about learning to value myself and my own well-being, and to let go of the belief that I deserved to be treated poorly. It was about recognizing that I was not responsible for the actions of my abuser, and that I had the power to take control of my own life and make choices that were in my best interest.

If you are currently struggling with the effects of emotional abuse, I want you to know that you are not alone. There are resources and support available to you, and it is possible to break free from the cycle of abuse and start the journey towards healing and forgiveness. It may not be an easy road, but it is one that is worth taking. You deserve to live a life free from fear, pain, and self-doubt, and I believe that with the right tools and support, you can get there.

Importance of forgiveness in healing from emotional abuse

The road to healing from emotional abuse can be long and difficult, but one powerful tool that can aid in the process is forgiveness. Forgiveness is a choice to let go of resentment and bitterness towards the person who has hurt you, and it can have a profound impact on your emotional well-being.

Forgiveness does not mean forgetting or excusing the behavior of the abuser. It is not about minimizing the harm they caused or reconciling with them. Rather, forgiveness is about releasing the anger and bitterness that you may be holding onto and finding peace within yourself.

Forgiveness is a process that begins with acknowledging the harm that was done to you. It requires confronting the pain and trauma head-on, and working through the emotions that come up as a result. This can be incredibly difficult, especially when you are dealing with the aftermath of emotional abuse. However, with the right support and resources, it is possible to make progress towards forgiveness and healing.

One of the biggest benefits of forgiveness is that it can free you from the cycle of anger and resentment that often accompanies emotional abuse. When you hold onto anger and bitterness towards your abuser, you are allowing them to continue to have power over you. By choosing to forgive, you are taking back that power and reclaiming control of your own life.

Forgiveness can also have a positive impact on your physical health. Holding onto anger and resentment can lead to increased stress and anxiety, which can have a negative impact on your overall well-being. By releasing those negative emotions through forgiveness, you may experience improvements in your physical health and well-being.

Another benefit of forgiveness is that it can help to rebuild relationships that have been damaged by emotional abuse. While it is not always possible or advisable to reconcile with your abuser, forgiveness can help you to repair relationships with other people in your life. When you release the negative emotions that are holding you back, you are better able to connect with others and build healthy, fulfilling relationships.

Of course, forgiveness is not always an easy process, and it may not be the right choice for everyone. It is important to take the time to explore your own emotions and feelings, and to work through any issues that may be holding you back. It may be helpful to seek out therapy or counseling, or to connect with a support group of other survivors of emotional abuse.

It is also important to remember that forgiveness is a personal choice, and that you should never feel pressured to forgive someone if it does not feel right for you. If forgiveness is something that you are considering, it is important to take the time to fully explore your own feelings and to make a decision that is right for you.

In conclusion, forgiveness can be a powerful tool in the healing process from emotional abuse. It can help to release the negative emotions that are holding you back, and to reclaim control of your own life. While forgiveness is not always easy, it is possible with the right support and resources. If you are struggling with the aftermath of emotional abuse, I encourage you to explore the possibility of forgiveness as a path towards healing and emotional well-being.

CHAPTER 2: UNDERSTANDING FORGIVENESS

❖ Definition of forgiveness and its misconceptions
❖ Benefits of forgiveness
❖ Different types of forgiveness
❖ The role of self-forgiveness in healing

In the previous chapter, we explored the impact of emotional abuse and the journey towards healing and forgiveness. Now, we will dive deeper into the concept of forgiveness itself. Forgiveness is a term that is often used in discussions of healing and recovery, but what does it actually mean? In this chapter, we will explore the definition of forgiveness, common misconceptions, the benefits of forgiveness, and the different types of forgiveness that exist.

Forgiveness is often defined as a conscious decision to release feelings of anger or resentment towards a person who has harmed you. It involves letting go of the desire for revenge or retribution and instead choosing to move forward with compassion and understanding. However, forgiveness is a complex process, and there are many misconceptions about what it involves.

One common misconception is that forgiveness means excusing or condoning the behavior of the person who hurt you. This is not the case. Forgiveness is not about minimizing the harm that was done or absolving the person of responsibility. Rather, it is about releasing the negative emotions that are holding you back and finding a sense of peace within yourself.

There are many benefits to forgiveness. Research has shown that forgiving others can lead to decreased feelings of anger, anxiety, and depression. It can also improve overall emotional well-being and increase resilience in the face of stress and adversity.

There are also different types of forgiveness, each of which involves a different process and outcome. Decisional forgiveness involves making a conscious decision to forgive, while emotional forgiveness involves actually experiencing the emotions associated with forgiveness, such as empathy and compassion. Conditional forgiveness involves setting certain conditions for forgiveness, while unconditional forgiveness involves forgiving without any conditions attached.

In addition to forgiving others, self-forgiveness is also an important aspect of the healing process. Self-forgiveness involves letting go of the blame and self-criticism that often accompanies feelings of guilt and shame. It is an important step towards self-compassion and self-acceptance.

Overall, forgiveness is a complex and multifaceted concept that plays an important role in the healing process from emotional abuse. In the following sections of this chapter, we will explore each aspect of forgiveness in more detail, and provide guidance on how to incorporate forgiveness into your own journey towards healing and emotional well-being.

"Forgiveness is not about forgetting or excusing the past, but about freeing ourselves from its grip and moving forward with compassion and understanding."

Definition of forgiveness and its misconceptions

Forgiveness is a term that is often used in discussions of healing and recovery, but what does it actually mean? In this section, we will explore the definition of forgiveness, common misconceptions, and the role that forgiveness plays in healing from emotional abuse.

Forgiveness is often defined as a conscious decision to release feelings of anger or resentment towards a person who has harmed you. It involves letting go of the desire for revenge or retribution and instead choosing to move forward with compassion and understanding. However, forgiveness is a complex process, and there are many misconceptions about what it involves.

One common misconception is that forgiveness means excusing or condoning the behavior of the person who hurt you. This is not the case. Forgiveness is not about minimizing the harm that was done or absolving the person of responsibility. Rather, it is about releasing the negative emotions that are holding you back and finding a sense of peace within yourself.

Another misconception about forgiveness is that it is a one-time event, a simple decision that can be made in a moment. In reality, forgiveness is often a long and difficult process that involves many stages. It requires a willingness to confront difficult emotions and memories, and to work through them in a constructive and healing way.

Furthermore, forgiveness does not necessarily mean reconciliation. While forgiveness can be an important step towards repairing a damaged relationship, it does not guarantee that the relationship will be restored to what it once was. It is possible to forgive someone without returning to the same level of closeness or trust.

It is important to note that forgiveness is a personal choice, and it may not be the right choice for everyone. Some people may choose to move on from the hurt without forgiving the person who caused it, and that is a valid choice. Forgiveness is not a requirement for healing, but it can be a powerful tool in the journey towards emotional well-being.

In conclusion, the definition of forgiveness is often misunderstood. It is not about excusing or minimizing harm, nor is it a one-time event. Rather, forgiveness is a complex and ongoing process that involves letting go of negative emotions and finding a sense of peace within yourself. It is a personal choice, and it may not be the right choice for everyone. In the following sections of this chapter, we will explore the benefits of forgiveness and the different types of forgiveness that exist.

Journal Exercises

❖ Write down your personal definition of forgiveness. What does forgiveness mean to you?

_____

_____

_____

_____

_____

_____

_____

_____

_____

❖ How do you think it can help you in your journey towards healing?

_____
_____
_____
_____
_____
_____
_____
_____
_____
_____

❖ Reflect on a time when you struggled to forgive someone who hurt you. What were some of the emotions that you experienced?

_____
_____
_____
_____
_____
_____
_____
_____
_____

❖ Did you have any misconceptions about forgiveness at the time?

_____
_____
_____
_____
_____

_____

_____

_____

_____

_____

❖ How did you eventually work through these feelings?

_____

_____

_____

_____

_____

_____

_____

_____

❖ Identify a misconception that you have held about forgiveness in the past. For example, you may have believed that forgiving someone meant that you had to forget what they did, or that forgiveness meant that you had to continue to have a relationship with that person. Write about how this misconception impacted your ability to forgive and move on from the hurt.

_____

_____

_____

_____

_____

_____

_____

_____

_____

❖ Write a letter to yourself from the perspective of
someone who has forgiven themselves or someone else.
What advice would they give you?

_____

_____

_____

_____

_____

_____

_____

_____

_____

❖ What kind of language would they use to encourage
and support you in your journey towards forgiveness?

_____

_____

_____

_____

_____

_____

_____

_____

_____

❖ Think about a situation where you have struggled to
forgive yourself. What are some of the negative beliefs
or self-talk patterns that are keeping you from forgiving
yourself?

_____

_____
_____
_____
_____
_____
_____
_____
_____
_____

❖ Write down some positive affirmations or reminders that you can use to challenge these beliefs and move towards self-forgiveness.

_____
_____
_____
_____
_____
_____
_____
_____
_____
_____

These exercises are designed to help you explore your own beliefs and experiences with forgiveness. Take your time with each exercise, and remember to be kind and compassionate with yourself throughout the process.

Benefits of forgiveness

Forgiveness is often viewed as a difficult and sometimes painful process, but it can bring with it a wide range of benefits that can help individuals heal and move forward from past hurts. In this chapter, we will explore some of the key benefits of forgiveness and how they can impact our lives.

Improved Mental Health

One of the most significant benefits of forgiveness is its positive impact on mental health. Studies have shown that forgiveness can reduce symptoms of anxiety, depression, and stress, while also increasing feelings of happiness and well-being. By letting go of anger and resentment towards those who have hurt us, we can free ourselves from the negative emotions that often hold us back and cause emotional distress.

Better Physical Health

The benefits of forgiveness extend beyond just mental health. Forgiveness has been shown to have a positive impact on physical health as well. Studies have found that people who forgive others have lower blood pressure, reduced levels of chronic pain, and improved immune function. By releasing feelings of anger and resentment, we can reduce the stress on our bodies, leading to improved overall health and well-being.

Improved Relationships

Forgiveness can also have a positive impact on our relationships with others. By choosing to forgive those who have hurt us, we can open the door to rebuilding and repairing damaged relationships. Forgiveness can foster increased understanding, empathy, and compassion, which can lead to stronger and more meaningful connections with others.

Increased Resilience

Forgiveness can also help individuals develop greater resilience in the face of adversity. By learning to forgive and move forward from past hurts, we can develop a greater sense of inner strength and resilience that can help us better cope with future challenges and setbacks. Forgiveness can help us learn to let go of negative emotions and focus on the present moment, which can lead to increased resilience and greater emotional flexibility.

Spiritual Growth

Forgiveness can also have a positive impact on spiritual growth and development. Many spiritual traditions emphasize the importance of forgiveness as a means of cultivating greater compassion, empathy, and understanding. By forgiving others and ourselves, we can deepen our connection to something greater than ourselves and foster greater spiritual growth and development.

Overall, the benefits of forgiveness are numerous and can have a significant impact on our lives. From improved mental and physical health to increased resilience and spiritual growth, forgiveness has the power to transform our lives in profound and meaningful ways. By embracing forgiveness as a key part of our healing journey, we can experience greater peace, happiness, and fulfillment in all areas of our lives.

"Forgiveness is not about forgetting. It is about letting go of another person's throat." - William Paul Young

Journal Exercises:

❖ Reflect on a time when you struggled to forgive someone. How did holding onto anger and resentment impact your mental and physical health?

_____
_____
_____
_____
_____
_____
_____
_____
_____

❖ How did it affect your relationships with others?

_____
_____
_____
_____
_____
_____
_____
_____

❖ Take some time to write about the emotions you experienced during this time and how you eventually were able to forgive.

_____
_____
_____
_____
_____

_____

_____

_____

_____

_____

❖ Think about a person you need to forgive in order to move forward with your life. Write a letter to this person, expressing your feelings of hurt, anger, and resentment.

_____

_____

_____

_____

_____

_____

_____

❖ Then, write a second letter, this time focusing on forgiveness and expressing your desire to let go of the past and move forward.

_____

_____

_____

_____

_____

_____

_____

_____

❖ Consider the benefits of forgiveness discussed in this chapter. Which benefit do you think would be the most impactful for you personally?

_____

_____

_____

_____

_____

_____

_____

_____

_____

❖ How can you begin to cultivate forgiveness in your life and reap these benefits?

_____

_____

_____

_____

_____

_____

_____

_____

❖ Write about your thoughts and feelings on this topic.

_____

_____

_____

_____

_____

_____

_____

Different types of forgiveness

Forgiveness is a complex and multifaceted concept that can take many different forms. While the ultimate goal of forgiveness is to let go of anger, bitterness, and resentment towards those who have hurt us, the path to forgiveness can look different for different people and situations. In this chapter, we will explore the different types of forgiveness and how they can be applied to various situations.

Decisional Forgiveness

The first type of forgiveness is decisional forgiveness. This form of forgiveness is a choice that we make to release our negative emotions towards someone who has wronged us. It is a conscious decision to let go of resentment and anger, regardless of whether the other person apologizes or accepts responsibility for their actions. This type of forgiveness does not require us to forget or excuse the other person's behavior, but rather to choose not to hold onto negative feelings towards them.

Emotional Forgiveness

Emotional forgiveness is a more complex form of forgiveness that involves a deeper healing process. This type of forgiveness requires us to work through our emotions and release the pain and hurt that we have been carrying. It involves acknowledging and processing our emotions, and eventually, moving towards a place of empathy and compassion for the person who hurt us. Emotional forgiveness may require time and effort, but it can ultimately lead to a more profound and lasting sense of peace and healing.

Conditional Forgiveness

Conditional forgiveness is a type of forgiveness that is contingent on certain conditions being met. For example, the person who wronged us may need to apologize or make amends in some way before we can fully forgive them. While conditional forgiveness can be a useful tool for setting boundaries and holding others accountable for their actions, it can also become a barrier to true forgiveness if the conditions are never met.

Self-Forgiveness

Self-forgiveness is another important form of forgiveness that is often overlooked. It involves accepting and forgiving ourselves for mistakes and shortcomings, rather than constantly punishing ourselves for past actions. Self-forgiveness can be especially challenging for those who have experienced emotional abuse, as they may have internalized the negative messages they received from their abuser. However, learning to forgive ourselves and let go of self-blame can be a powerful step towards healing and growth.

It is important to note that forgiveness is not a one-size-fits-all process. Different types of forgiveness may be more appropriate for different situations, and each person's journey towards forgiveness will be unique. However, regardless of the type of forgiveness we choose to pursue, the act of forgiveness can be incredibly powerful and transformative.

By choosing to forgive, we free ourselves from the burden of anger and resentment, and create space for healing, growth, and new beginnings.

"Forgiveness is not a one-size-fits-all solution. It comes in different shapes and sizes, but they all have one thing in common - the power to heal."

Journal exercises:

❖ Reflect on a time when you forgave someone for a wrongdoing. Was it a quick or gradual process?

_____

_____

_____

_____

_____

_____

_____

_____

_____

❖ What did it feel like to let go of the anger and resentment?

_____

_____

_____

_____

_____

_____

_____

_____

_____

❖ How did forgiveness benefit you?

_____
_____
_____
_____
_____
_____
_____
_____
_____

❖ Consider the different types of forgiveness discussed in this chapter - decisional, emotional, and deep forgiveness. Which type(s) do you find most challenging?

_____
_____
_____
_____
_____
_____
_____
_____

❖ Why?

_____
_____
_____
_____
_____

_____

_____

_____

_____

_____

❖ How might you work towards practicing these types of forgiveness in your life?

_____

_____

_____

_____

_____

_____

_____

_____

❖ Think about a past hurt or betrayal that you have not been able to forgive. Are there any misconceptions about forgiveness that might be holding you back?

_____

_____

_____

_____

_____

_____

_____

_____

❖ How might you reframe your understanding of forgiveness in a way that feels more empowering and aligned with your personal values?

_____

_____

_____

_____

_____

_____

_____

_____

_____

❖ Write a letter to yourself or someone you have wronged, expressing your decision to forgive and release any negative emotions attached to the situation. Alternatively, write a letter to someone who has wronged you, but do not send it. Instead, reflect on how this exercise has impacted your perspective on forgiveness and the potential for healing.

_____

_____

_____

_____

_____

_____

_____

_____

_____

_____

_____

The role of self-forgiveness in healing

The concept of forgiveness is often associated with letting go of negative emotions towards others who have wronged us. However, it is equally important to extend that same compassion and understanding towards ourselves. Self-forgiveness is a crucial component of the healing process from emotional abuse, as it allows us to let go of self-blame and shame and move towards a place of self-acceptance and love. In this chapter, we will explore the role of self-forgiveness in healing and provide strategies for cultivating self-forgiveness in our lives.

Definition of Self-Forgiveness

Self-forgiveness is the act of releasing ourselves from self-blame and self-criticism for past mistakes, failures, or shortcomings. It is the recognition that we are imperfect beings who are capable of making mistakes and that these mistakes do not define our worth or value as human beings. Self-forgiveness involves taking responsibility for our actions, acknowledging the impact they may have had on ourselves and others, and choosing to move forward with self-compassion and understanding.

Barriers to Self-Forgiveness

Self-forgiveness can be a difficult and challenging process, as it requires us to confront our own shortcomings and accept our vulnerabilities. There are several barriers that can hinder our ability to forgive ourselves, including:

- ❖ Shame and guilt - Feelings of shame and guilt can often consume us, making it difficult to move forward and let go of negative self-judgment.

- ❖ Perfectionism - The belief that we must be perfect and any mistake is a failure can lead to self-criticism and self-blame.

- ❖ Fear of vulnerability - Opening ourselves up to forgiveness requires vulnerability and trust, which can be scary and uncomfortable.

- ❖ Lack of self-compassion - A lack of self-compassion can make it difficult to extend forgiveness to ourselves, as we may not believe we deserve it.

Benefits of Self-Forgiveness

Practicing self-forgiveness has numerous benefits for our mental and emotional well-being. When we forgive ourselves, we:

- ❖ Reduce stress and anxiety - By releasing ourselves from the burden of self-blame and self-criticism, we can experience a greater sense of inner peace and calm.

- ❖ Improve self-esteem - Forgiving ourselves allows us to recognize our own worth and value, which can improve our self-esteem and confidence.

- ❖ Strengthen relationships - When we forgive ourselves, we are better able to extend forgiveness to others and strengthen our relationships.

❖ Promote resilience - Self-forgiveness allows us to bounce back from setbacks and failures, promoting resilience and adaptability.

❖ Strategies for Cultivating Self-Forgiveness
Cultivating self-forgiveness is a process that requires patience, self-compassion, and a willingness to let go of negative self-judgment. Here are some strategies that can help us practice self-forgiveness:

❖ Practice mindfulness - Mindfulness can help us cultivate self-awareness and non-judgmental self-acceptance, which are essential components of self-forgiveness.

❖ Challenge negative self-talk - When we notice negative self-talk, we can challenge it by asking ourselves if it is based in reality, and if not, replace it with a more positive and compassionate perspective.

❖ Practice self-care - Practicing self-care, such as getting enough sleep, exercise, and healthy food, can help us feel better about ourselves and promote self-compassion.

❖ Seek support - Talking to a trusted friend, family member, or therapist can provide us with a supportive space to process our emotions and gain perspective on our situation.

In conclusion, self-forgiveness is a critical component of the healing process from emotional abuse. By cultivating self-compassion, releasing self-blame and negative self-judgment, and acknowledging our own humanity, we can begin to let go of the shame and self-loathing that can keep us trapped in the cycle of emotional abuse. Here are some additional tips for practicing self-forgiveness and cultivating self-compassion:

❖ Practice mindfulness: Mindfulness is the practice of being present in the moment and observing our thoughts and feelings without judgment. By cultivating mindfulness, we can become more aware of our negative self-talk and begin to challenge it with self-compassion.

❖ Use affirmations: Affirmations are positive statements that we repeat to ourselves to counteract negative self-talk. By using affirmations such as "I am worthy of love and respect" or "I forgive myself for past mistakes," we can begin to rewire our brains to think more positively about ourselves.

❖ Practice self-care: Self-care is the practice of taking care of our physical, emotional, and mental well-being. By prioritizing self-care activities such as exercise, healthy eating, and engaging in hobbies that bring us joy, we can increase our self-esteem and sense of self-worth.

❖ Seek support: Healing from emotional abuse is a journey, and it is essential to seek support along the way. This can include therapy, support groups, or trusted friends and family members who can provide a listening ear and a supportive presence.

By practicing self-forgiveness and cultivating self-compassion, we can break free from the cycle of emotional abuse and begin to live a life of healing and wholeness. It is not an easy journey, but it is a journey that is worth taking for our own well-being and happiness.

In conclusion, healing from emotional abuse is a complex and challenging process that requires time, patience, and self-compassion. By understanding the nature of emotional abuse, the importance of forgiveness, and the critical role of self-forgiveness in the healing process, we can begin to take the necessary steps towards a life of healing and wholeness. Remember that healing is a journey, and it is a journey that is unique to each person. Be gentle with yourself, seek support, and know that with time and patience, healing is possible.

"Forgiving yourself is the ultimate act of self-love and healing. You deserve the same compassion and kindness you offer to others."

Journal Exercises:

❖ Write a letter of self-forgiveness to yourself. Start by acknowledging the things that you have done or thought that you regret or feel guilty about. Then, write a message to yourself that shows compassion, kindness, and forgiveness. Remind yourself that you are not defined by your mistakes and that you are worthy of forgiveness and healing.

_____

_____

_____

_____

_____

_____

_____

_____

_____

_____

_____

❖ Identify the self-critical voices in your mind. Take a few minutes to reflect on the negative self-talk that you often engage in. Write down those thoughts and try to identify where they come from. Ask yourself if they are serving you in any way, or if they are hindering your healing process. Then, challenge those thoughts by writing down a counter-argument that is more compassionate and forgiving.

_____

_____

_____

_____

_____

_____

_____

_____

_____

❖ Practice self-compassion. Choose a self-compassion practice that resonates with you and make it a part of your daily routine. This could be as simple as giving yourself a hug or placing your hand on your heart and saying kind words to yourself. You could also try meditation or other mindfulness practices that promote self-compassion. Remember, the more you practice self-compassion, the more you will be able to forgive yourself and move towards healing.

In conclusion, forgiveness is a powerful tool that can help us heal from the emotional wounds inflicted by others, as well as those we inflict upon ourselves. However, it is important to understand that forgiveness is not a one-size-fits-all solution, and that different types of forgiveness may be needed depending on the situation.

We must also recognize the misconceptions surrounding forgiveness, such as the idea that forgiveness means forgetting or condoning the behavior of the person who harmed us. In reality, forgiveness is about releasing ourselves from the negative emotions and effects of the harm, not absolving the person of responsibility for their actions.

Furthermore, self-forgiveness is an essential aspect of the healing process. It involves cultivating self-compassion, releasing self-blame and negative self-judgment, and acknowledging that we are all human and make mistakes.

By embracing forgiveness, we can free ourselves from the weight of anger, resentment, and bitterness, and start the journey towards healing and wholeness. We can learn to let go of the past and move forward with a renewed sense of hope, strength, and resilience.

Remember, forgiveness is not always easy, but it is always possible. It takes time, patience, and courage to forgive, but the benefits of doing so are immeasurable. May we all find the courage to embrace forgiveness and start the journey towards healing and rising strong.

CHAPTER 3: THE POWER OF STORYTELLING

- ❖ The therapeutic benefits of sharing personal stories
- ❖ Survivor stories of overcoming emotional abuse and forgiving abusers
- ❖ The importance of listening and validating others' stories

Stories have the power to heal. They allow us to connect with others, to share our experiences, and to find validation and understanding in a world that can often feel isolating and overwhelming. When it comes to healing from emotional abuse, storytelling can be a powerful tool.

In this chapter, we will explore the therapeutic benefits of sharing personal stories, both for the storyteller and for the listener. We will hear survivor stories of overcoming emotional abuse and forgiving abusers, and we will discuss the importance of listening and validating others' stories.

Through the sharing and receiving of stories, we can find hope, healing, and connection.

The therapeutic benefits of sharing personal stories

As survivors of emotional abuse, we often carry the weight of our experiences with us, feeling as though we are alone in our struggles. It can be difficult to open up to others about our experiences, especially when we fear judgment or invalidation. However, the act of sharing our personal stories can be incredibly therapeutic and healing.

When we share our stories with others, we begin to release the shame and isolation that often accompanies experiences of emotional abuse. We find validation and understanding in the listening ear of a trusted friend or therapist. We realize that we are not alone, and that others have experienced similar struggles.

Sharing our stories also allows us to process our experiences in a new way. As we tell our stories, we gain new insights and perspectives on our experiences. We may see patterns or themes that we hadn't noticed before. We may find new meaning or purpose in our struggles.

Furthermore, telling our stories can help us to reclaim our power and agency. When we have experienced emotional abuse, we may feel as though our abuser has taken away our ability to speak our truth or make choices for ourselves. By sharing our stories, we take back some of that power. We choose to speak our truth and share our experiences, despite any fears or doubts we may have.

Of course, the act of sharing our stories can also be incredibly vulnerable and scary. It requires us to be honest and open, even when we feel ashamed or embarrassed. It can be helpful to start small, by sharing our experiences with a trusted friend or therapist. Over time, we may feel more comfortable sharing our stories with a wider audience.

It's important to note that sharing our stories doesn't necessarily mean we have to forgive our abuser or forget what happened to us. We can share our stories as a way of processing our experiences and finding healing, without necessarily needing to reconcile with our abuser.

In fact, sharing our stories can be a powerful form of resistance and activism. When we speak out about our experiences, we raise awareness about the prevalence of emotional abuse and the need for support and resources for survivors. We help to break down the stigma and shame that can keep us silent and isolated.

Overall, sharing our personal stories can be an incredibly therapeutic and healing experience. It allows us to release shame and isolation, process our experiences in new ways, reclaim our power and agency, and raise awareness about the need for support and resources for survivors of emotional abuse.

"Owning our story can be hard but not nearly as difficult as spending our lives running from it." - Brené Brown

Journal Exercises:

❖ Reflect on a time when you shared a personal story with someone and how it made you feel. Did it provide a sense of relief or release?

_____
_____
_____
_____
_____
_____
_____
_____
_____
_____

❖ Did it help you connect with the other person on a deeper level?

_____

_____

_____

_____

_____

_____

_____

_____

_____

❖ Think about a personal story that you have been hesitant to share with others. Write down what is holding you back from sharing and how you think it would feel to finally let it out.

_____

_____

_____

_____

_____

_____

_____

_____

_____

❖ Write down a list of people in your life that you trust and feel comfortable sharing personal stories with.

_____

_____

_____

_____

_____

_____

_____

_____

_____

❖ Make a plan to reach out to at least one of them this week and share something that you have been holding onto.

_____

_____

_____

_____

_____

_____

_____

_____

❖ Reflect on how it feels to open up and connect with another person.

_____

_____

_____

_____

_____

_____

_____

_____

_____

Survivor stories of overcoming emotional abuse and forgiving abusers

My name is Saira, and for years I was trapped in a cycle of emotional abuse. My husband, whom I had thought was my soulmate, had gradually become more and more controlling. He would criticize my every move and belittle my accomplishments. Even worse, he would twist my words and make me doubt my own memory, leaving me feeling confused and unsure of myself.

It took me a long time to realize that what I was experiencing was emotional abuse. I had always thought abuse meant physical violence, but the bruises on my heart were just as real as any physical injury. Eventually, I found the strength to leave him and start rebuilding my life.

But the journey towards healing and forgiveness was a long and difficult one. I struggled with self-doubt and a deep-seated belief that I didn't deserve happiness. It wasn't until I started sharing my story with others that I began to see the healing power of storytelling.

Through sharing my experiences with fellow survivors, I realized that I was not alone. I saw the strength and resilience of others who had faced similar traumas and come out the other side. Their stories gave me hope and inspiration, and I began to see that forgiveness was not just possible, but necessary for my own healing.

It wasn't easy, but with the help of therapy and the support of my loved ones, I started to forgive my ex-husband. It wasn't about excusing his behavior, but rather freeing myself from the burden of anger and resentment. Forgiveness was the key to letting go of the past and moving forward with my life.

Now, years later, I am in a much better place. I have a new partner who loves and respects me for who I am, and I have a sense of peace and self-worth that I never thought possible. Through sharing my story and listening to others, I have learned that healing is a journey, but one that is possible for anyone who has the courage to take the first step.
-Saira

Growing up, I always knew I was different. I didn't fit into the mold that society had created for me, and that made me feel like an outsider. It wasn't until I came out as a member of the LGBT+ community that things really started to change for me. While I was lucky to have some supportive friends and family members, others weren't so accepting.

One person in particular was my father. He couldn't accept that his child was "different," and he made it known in every way possible. He would belittle me, tell me that I was going to hell, and even physically abuse me at times. It was a nightmare that I couldn't seem to escape.

As I got older, I realized that I had two options: let my father's abuse continue to control my life, or find a way to break free. I chose the latter. I sought out therapy and support groups for LGBT+ individuals, and slowly but surely, I began to rebuild my sense of self-worth.

It wasn't easy. There were moments where I felt like giving up, like the weight of my father's words and actions would never truly leave me. But over time, I learned that forgiveness was the key to my own healing. It wasn't about excusing my father's behavior or pretending like it never happened, but about letting go of the anger and resentment that had been eating away at me for so long.

The process of forgiveness wasn't quick or easy, but it was worth it. It allowed me to see my father as a flawed human being, rather than a monster. It allowed me to acknowledge the pain that he had caused me, while also recognizing that he too was a victim of societal conditioning and ignorance.

Today, I am proud to say that I have forgiven my father. It's not something that happened overnight, but rather a gradual journey towards healing and acceptance. Forgiveness has allowed me to move forward with my life, and to let go of the emotional baggage that was holding me back.

If there's one thing I want other survivors of emotional abuse to know, it's that forgiveness is possible. It's not a magic cure-all, but it is a powerful tool for healing and reclaiming your sense of self-worth.
-Phoenix

The importance of listening and validating others' stories

The power of storytelling and sharing personal experiences can be a critical part of healing from emotional abuse. However, it is not just the act of sharing one's story that is important, but also the act of listening and validating the stories of others. When we listen and validate the stories of others, we create a safe and supportive space for healing and growth. In this chapter, we will explore the importance of listening and validating others' stories, and how this can be a transformative experience for both the storyteller and the listener.

Listening to others' stories can be a challenging task, especially if those stories involve experiences of trauma and abuse. It can be uncomfortable to hear about someone else's pain and suffering, and it can be tempting to try to fix or minimize their experiences. However, this is not helpful or healing for the storyteller. Instead, what is needed is a space for the story to be heard and acknowledged, without judgment or interruption.

Validation is an essential part of this process. When we validate someone's story, we are acknowledging their experiences and feelings as real and valid. We are not trying to change or fix anything, but simply offering support and empathy. Validation can help the storyteller to feel heard and understood, and can help to build trust and connection between the storyteller and listener.

For the listener, the act of listening and validating someone else's story can also be transformative. It can help us to develop empathy and compassion, and to understand the impact of emotional abuse on others. It can also help us to recognize and acknowledge our own biases and assumptions, and to challenge them in a meaningful way.

There are many different ways that we can listen and validate others' stories. One important way is to create a safe and supportive space for sharing. This can be done by being present and attentive, and by avoiding judgment or interruption. It can also be helpful to offer words of validation and support, such as "I believe you" or "I'm here for you."

Another important aspect of listening and validating others' stories is to recognize the courage and strength of the storyteller. Sharing personal experiences of trauma and abuse is not an easy task, and it takes a great deal of bravery to do so. By acknowledging and honoring this courage, we can help to build trust and connection, and to create a safe and supportive environment for healing and growth.

It is important to note that listening and validating others' stories does not mean that we have to agree with everything that is said. It is possible to validate someone's experiences and feelings while still maintaining our own boundaries and perspectives. The key is to approach the process with empathy and openness, and to offer support and validation in a way that feels authentic and genuine.

In conclusion, the act of listening and validating others' stories can be a transformative experience for both the storyteller and the listener. It can help to create a safe and supportive space for healing and growth, and can help us to develop empathy, compassion, and understanding. By recognizing the importance of listening and validating others' stories, we can help to break down barriers and build connections, and create a more compassionate and supportive world.

"Listening is a gift we give to others. Validating their stories is a gift we give to ourselves." - Unknown

Journal Exercises:

❖ Reflect on a time when someone listened to you and validated your story. How did it make you feel?

_____

_____

_____

_____

_____

_____

_____

_____

_____

❖ How did it impact your healing process?

_____

_____

_____

_____

_____

_____

_____

_____

_____

❖ Think about a time when you didn't feel heard or validated in sharing your story. How did it make you feel?

_____

_____

_____

_____

_____

_____

_____

_____

_____

_____

_____

❖   Did it affect your willingness to share your story in the future?

_____

_____

_____

_____

_____

_____

_____

_____

_____

_____

❖   Consider the people in your life who may have experienced emotional abuse or other forms of trauma. How can you be a better listener and validate their stories?

_____

_____

_____

_____

_____

_____

_____

_____

_____

❖ How might this impact their healing process?

_____
_____
_____
_____
_____
_____
_____
_____
_____
_____

❖ Write about a time when you listened to and validated someone else's story. How did it feel to be able to offer that support?

_____
_____
_____
_____
_____
_____
_____
_____
_____

❖ Did it deepen your connection with that person?

_____
_____
_____
_____
_____
_____
_____

_____

_____

_____

_____

❖ Reflect on the quote above. How can listening and
   validating others' stories be a gift to ourselves?

_____

_____

_____

_____

_____

_____

_____

_____

❖ How might it impact our own healing and growth?

_____

_____

_____

_____

_____

_____

_____

_____

CHAPTER 4: THE PROCESS OF FORGIVENESS

❖ The stages of forgiveness
❖ Practical exercises for fostering forgiveness
❖ Common obstacles to forgiveness and how to overcome them

Forgiveness is a process that can take time and effort, but it is a critical step in healing from emotional abuse. In this chapter, we will explore the stages of forgiveness and provide practical exercises to help you on your journey. We will also address common obstacles to forgiveness and provide strategies for overcoming them. Remember, forgiveness is not about excusing the behavior of the abuser or forgetting what has happened, but about releasing the hold that the pain and resentment has on your life. By working through the process of forgiveness, you can reclaim your power and move towards a brighter future.

The stages of forgiveness

Forgiveness is not a single event, but rather a process that takes time and effort. It involves a series of stages that a person goes through to fully let go of the hurt, anger, and resentment caused by someone else's actions. While there is no one-size-fits-all formula for forgiveness, understanding the stages involved can help individuals navigate the process more effectively.

Stage 1: Acknowledgment of the Hurt

The first stage of forgiveness is acknowledging the hurt caused by the offender. This involves fully accepting the pain that was inflicted and recognizing the impact it had on one's life. Often, people try to push away their emotions or downplay the severity of the situation, but this can hinder the forgiveness process. It's important to allow oneself to feel the pain and acknowledge the emotions that come with it.

Stage 2: Anger and Resentment

The next stage is characterized by feelings of anger and resentment towards the offender. This is a natural reaction to the pain that was inflicted and can be difficult to overcome. However, it's important to remember that holding onto anger and resentment only harms oneself and prevents the healing process. In this stage, it's important to express and process these emotions in a healthy way, such as through journaling, talking with a trusted friend, or seeking therapy.

Stage 3: Empathy and Understanding

In this stage, a person begins to see the situation from the offender's perspective and seeks to understand why they acted in the way they did. This does not mean excusing or justifying the behavior, but rather recognizing that the offender may have had their own pain or struggles that contributed to their actions. This stage requires an open mind and a willingness to consider different perspectives.

Stage 4: Acceptance and Release

The fourth stage of forgiveness involves accepting the situation for what it is and letting go of the negative emotions associated with it. This does not mean forgetting what happened or pretending that it didn't hurt, but rather releasing the grip that the hurt has on one's life. This can involve choosing to no longer dwell on the past, practicing self-care and self-compassion, and actively working towards a more positive future.

Stage 5: Reconciliation or Moving On

The final stage of forgiveness is either reconciling with the offender or moving on without them. This stage is not always necessary or possible, but can provide a sense of closure and resolution. Reconciliation involves rebuilding trust and repairing the relationship, while moving on involves letting go of the relationship and finding closure in oneself.

The stages of forgiveness are not always linear, and a person may move back and forth between stages as they navigate the process. It's important to give oneself grace and patience as forgiveness is a deeply personal journey.

In the next section, we will explore practical exercises for fostering forgiveness and overcoming common obstacles that can arise during the forgiveness process.

"Forgiveness is not a one-time event, it is a process. Each stage is a step towards healing and freedom." - Unknown

Journal exercises:

❖ Reflection: Take some time to reflect on a situation in your life where forgiveness may be needed. Write down your thoughts and feelings about the situation, and what you hope to achieve through forgiveness.

_____

_____

_____

_____

_____

_____

_____

_____

_____

❖ Acknowledge the hurt: In order to move through the stages of forgiveness, it's important to acknowledge the hurt that has been caused. Write a letter to yourself or the person who hurt you, acknowledging the pain and harm that was caused.

_____

_____

_____

_____

_____

_____

_____

_____

❖ Empathy: Try to put yourself in the shoes of the person who hurt you. Write down what you think might have led them to behave the way they did. This exercise can help you gain empathy and understanding for the other person.

_____

_____

_____

_____

_____

_____

_____

_____

_____

_____

❖ Decision: Make a decision to forgive. Write down your reasons for wanting to forgive and what you hope to gain from the process.

_____

_____

_____

_____

_____

_____

_____

_____

_____

_____

❖ Action: Take action towards forgiveness. This can include reaching out to the person who hurt you, seeking therapy, or practicing self-forgiveness. Write down the steps you plan to take and commit to taking action towards forgiveness.

Practical exercises for fostering forgiveness

Forgiveness is a process that takes time and effort, but it can be achieved through practical exercises. While it is easier said than done, with consistent effort, individuals can overcome the hurt and pain caused by emotional abuse and choose to forgive. In this chapter, we will explore some practical exercises for fostering forgiveness and help individuals take the necessary steps towards healing.

Practice Self-Compassion

The first step towards forgiveness is to extend compassion to oneself. Self-compassion is the practice of treating oneself with kindness, care, and understanding. Often, individuals who have experienced emotional abuse tend to blame themselves for the actions of their abusers. This self-blame only exacerbates their pain and makes it harder to forgive.

To practice self-compassion, start by acknowledging the pain and hurt caused by the abuse. It is essential to recognize that it was not your fault and that you deserve to be treated with love and respect. Use positive affirmations to remind yourself that you are worthy of forgiveness and that you are doing your best to heal.

Write a Forgiveness Letter

Writing a forgiveness letter can be a powerful exercise in releasing pent-up emotions and letting go of resentment. This exercise involves writing a letter to the abuser expressing forgiveness and releasing any negative feelings towards them. It is important to note that this letter is for personal growth and healing and does not require sending it to the abuser.

Begin by writing down your thoughts and feelings about the abuse and the impact it had on your life. Next, write a letter to the abuser expressing forgiveness for their actions and releasing any negative feelings towards them. It is important to be honest and authentic in this letter and to write from a place of compassion and understanding.

Use Guided Meditation

Guided meditation can be an effective tool for fostering forgiveness. Meditation helps individuals to quiet their minds and focus on the present moment. It can help to release negative thoughts and emotions, making room for forgiveness.

Find a quiet and peaceful place where you can meditate without distractions. Set a timer for 10-15 minutes and close your eyes. Focus on your breath and bring your attention to your body. Imagine a peaceful and safe environment, like a garden or a beach. Picture yourself in this environment and let go of any negative thoughts and emotions. Allow yourself to feel the emotions that arise and offer yourself compassion and forgiveness.

Seek Professional Help

Forgiveness is a complex process, and it is important to seek professional help if needed. Therapy can be an effective tool for individuals struggling to forgive. A therapist can help individuals work through their emotions and provide support throughout the forgiveness process.

Therapy can also help individuals to identify and address any underlying issues that may be hindering their ability to forgive. A therapist can help individuals develop coping strategies and provide tools for managing difficult emotions.

Practice Gratitude

Gratitude is the practice of recognizing and appreciating the good things in life. Practicing gratitude can help individuals to shift their focus from the negative to the positive. It can help to cultivate a sense of peace and contentment, making forgiveness easier to achieve.

Take a few minutes each day to reflect on the things in life that you are grateful for. Write them down in a journal or simply reflect on them in your mind. Focus on the positive aspects of life and try to let go of negative thoughts and emotions.

In conclusion, forgiveness is a process that takes time and effort, but it can be achieved through practical exercises. By practicing self-compassion, writing a forgiveness letter, using guided meditation, seeking professional help, and practicing gratitude, individuals can take the necessary steps towards forgiveness and healing. Remember, forgiveness is not about forgetting the past or excusing harmful behavior. It is about choosing to let go of the negative emotions and moving forward in a positive direction.

Here are some additional practical exercises for fostering forgiveness:

Engage in self-reflection: Spend some time reflecting on your own actions and the role you may have played in the situation. Consider how your own behavior may have impacted the relationship and whether there are any actions you can take to make amends.

Practice empathy: Try to put yourself in the shoes of the person who hurt you. Consider what they may have been going through at the time and try to understand their perspective. This can help you to see the situation from a different angle and may make it easier to forgive them.

Seek out positive role models: Look for people in your life who embody forgiveness and try to learn from them. This could be a friend, family member, or even a public figure who inspires you.

Set boundaries: Forgiveness does not mean that you have to continue to have a relationship with the person who hurt you. It is important to set boundaries that will help to protect your emotional well-being and ensure that you are not put in a position to be hurt again.

Practice mindfulness: Mindfulness can be a powerful tool in the forgiveness process. By staying present in the moment and focusing on your breath, you can cultivate a sense of calm and clarity that can help you to let go of negative emotions.

Write a gratitude journal: Take some time each day to write down a few things that you are grateful for. This can help to shift your focus away from negative emotions and towards the positive aspects of your life.

Remember, forgiveness is a journey and it may take time to fully let go of negative emotions. Be patient with yourself and know that each step you take towards forgiveness is a step towards healing.

In the next section, we will explore some common obstacles to forgiveness and strategies for overcoming them.

Common obstacles to forgiveness and how to overcome them

Forgiveness is a journey that involves confronting and overcoming various obstacles. These obstacles can be internal or external, and they can present significant challenges to the process of forgiveness. In this chapter, we will explore some of the common obstacles to forgiveness and how to overcome them.

Anger and Resentment

Anger and resentment are natural emotional responses to the pain and hurt caused by emotional abuse. However, holding onto these emotions can hinder the process of forgiveness. Anger and resentment can prevent individuals from letting go of their pain and moving forward.

To overcome anger and resentment, it is essential to acknowledge these emotions and their underlying causes. Practice mindfulness techniques to observe and accept these emotions, without judgment. Reframe negative thoughts and feelings by reminding yourself that forgiveness is a process and not an event. Express your emotions in a healthy and safe way by journaling, speaking to a trusted friend or therapist, or participating in anger management therapy.

Fear of vulnerability

Forgiveness requires vulnerability, which can be challenging for some individuals, especially those who have experienced emotional abuse. The fear of being hurt again, opening up old wounds, or being rejected can prevent individuals from practicing forgiveness.

To overcome the fear of vulnerability, it is essential to acknowledge and accept the risk of being vulnerable. Recognize that vulnerability is a strength, not a weakness. Practice self-compassion and remind yourself that it is okay to make mistakes and be imperfect. Work on building healthy boundaries and setting limits to protect yourself from further harm.

Resistance to change

Some individuals may resist forgiveness because it requires change and growth. Forgiveness involves letting go of old ways of thinking and behaving, which can be uncomfortable for some individuals.

To overcome resistance to change, it is essential to recognize the benefits of forgiveness and the cost of holding onto negative emotions. Focus on the positive outcomes of forgiveness, such as emotional healing, freedom from anger and resentment, and improved relationships. Practice self-awareness and identify areas in your life where change is needed. Take small steps towards change and celebrate your progress along the way.

Lack of empathy

Lack of empathy towards the offender can prevent individuals from practicing forgiveness. It can be difficult to see things from the perspective of someone who has caused pain and hurt.

To overcome a lack of empathy, it is essential to practice empathy towards oneself and others. Cultivate self-compassion and acknowledge your own pain and hurt caused by emotional abuse. Practice active listening and try to understand the perspective of the offender. Seek out therapy or support groups to learn strategies for developing empathy.

Misconceptions about forgiveness

Finally, misconceptions about forgiveness can prevent individuals from practicing forgiveness. Some may believe that forgiveness means forgetting or condoning the offender's behavior, or that forgiveness requires reconciliation.

To overcome misconceptions about forgiveness, it is essential to learn about the true meaning of forgiveness. Recognize that forgiveness is a process that involves acknowledging the pain and hurt caused by emotional abuse, letting go of negative emotions, and creating space for healing. Forgiveness does not require forgetting, condoning, or reconciliation, but rather it is a personal decision to release negative emotions and move forward.

In conclusion, forgiveness is a process that can be hindered by various obstacles. Anger and resentment, fear of vulnerability, resistance to change, lack of empathy, and misconceptions about forgiveness can all present significant challenges to the process of forgiveness. However, by acknowledging and accepting these obstacles, practicing self-compassion, cultivating empathy, and reframing negative thoughts and feelings, individuals can take the necessary steps towards forgiveness and healing.

"Forgiveness does not erase the past, but it can help to rewrite the future."

Journal Exercises:

- ❖ Write about a time when you struggled to forgive someone.

_____
_____
_____
_____
_____
_____
_____
_____

_____

❖ What were the obstacles that prevented you from forgiving them?

_____
_____
_____
_____
_____
_____
_____
_____
_____

❖ How did you feel about the situation? Write about how you eventually overcame these obstacles and found forgiveness.

❖ Think about someone in your life who you are currently having trouble forgiving. Write a letter to them expressing your feelings, but do not send it. Use this letter as a way to process your emotions and work towards forgiveness.

_____
_____
_____
_____
_____
_____
_____
_____
_____
_____
_____

_____

_____

_____

_____

_____

_____

_____

_____

_____

❖ Reflect on the ways in which you have forgiven others in the past. What techniques or strategies have worked for you?

_____

_____

_____

_____

_____

_____

_____

_____

❖ Write about how you can apply these strategies to your current situation.

_____

_____

_____

_____

_____

_____

_____

_____

❖ Identify any negative self-talk or limiting beliefs that may be preventing you from forgiving someone. Write about how you can reframe these thoughts to be more compassionate and forgiving.

_____
_____
_____
_____
_____
_____
_____
_____
_____

❖ Think about a time when someone forgave you for something you did. How did that make you feel?

_____
_____
_____
_____
_____
_____
_____
_____

❖ Write about how you can use that experience to motivate yourself to forgive others.

_____
_____

_____

_____

_____

_____

_____

_____

_____

_____

_____

In conclusion, forgiveness is a complex process that requires time, effort, and self-reflection. It is not always easy, and there may be obstacles that seem insurmountable. However, by understanding the stages of forgiveness, practicing practical exercises, and acknowledging and working through common obstacles, individuals can begin the journey towards healing and forgiveness.

It is important to remember that forgiveness is not about excusing or forgetting the harm that was done, but rather releasing the hold that the hurt has on our lives. It is a way of taking back control and finding peace within ourselves, even if the other person involved is not willing to participate in the process.

By committing to forgiveness, we can move towards a more positive and fulfilling future, free from the weight of anger, resentment, and pain. It is not an easy path, but with patience, compassion, and perseverance, it is a path that can lead to a life of greater happiness, inner peace, and self-acceptance.

CHAPTER 5: UPLIFTING QUOTES AND AFFIRMATIONS

❖ Inspirational quotes about forgiveness and healing
❖ Affirmations for self-compassion and self-love

Chapter 5 is all about uplifting and empowering quotes and affirmations to help you on your journey towards forgiveness and healing from emotional abuse. Sometimes, we need a little extra encouragement and support, and these quotes and affirmations can serve as a reminder that we are capable of overcoming our past and creating a better future for ourselves. Whether you need a boost of self-confidence or a reminder to be kind to yourself, these quotes and affirmations are here to lift you up and remind you of your worth. So take a deep breath, and let's dive into some inspiring words that will help you on your path towards healing.

Inspirational quotes about forgiveness and healing

Inspirational quotes can be a powerful tool for providing comfort, hope, and motivation to those who are on the journey of forgiveness and healing. Here are some inspirational quotes about forgiveness and healing that can provide encouragement and inspiration along the way.

"Forgiveness is not a feeling; it's a decision we make because we want to do what's right before God. It's a quality decision that won't be easy and it may take time to get through the process, but we can do it with God's help." - Joyce Meyer

This quote reminds us that forgiveness is a choice that we make, and that it can be a difficult process. However, with faith and determination, we can overcome the obstacles and move towards healing.

"Forgiveness is the fragrance that the violet sheds on the heel that has crushed it." - Mark Twain

This beautiful metaphor reminds us that forgiveness has the power to transform even the most painful experiences into something beautiful and fragrant.

"The weak can never forgive. Forgiveness is the attribute of the strong." - Mahatma Gandhi

This quote challenges us to see forgiveness not as a sign of weakness, but as a sign of strength and resilience.

"Forgive others, not because they deserve forgiveness, but because you deserve peace." - Jonathan Lockwood Huie

This quote highlights the importance of forgiveness not only for the benefit of others, but also for our own well-being and inner peace.

"Forgiveness does not change the past, but it does enlarge the future." - Paul Boese

This quote reminds us that forgiveness is not about erasing or forgetting the past, but rather about creating a brighter and more hopeful future for ourselves.

"The practice of forgiveness is our most important contribution to the healing of the world." - Marianne Williamson

This quote reminds us that forgiveness is not just a personal journey, but also a way of contributing to the healing of our communities and the world around us.

"Forgiveness is giving up the hope that the past could have been any different." - Oprah Winfrey

This quote challenges us to let go of our regrets and wishes for a different past, and to focus instead on creating a more positive and empowered future.

"True forgiveness is when you can say, 'Thank you for that experience.'" - Oprah Winfrey

This quote encourages us to see even the most painful experiences as opportunities for growth, learning, and ultimately, gratitude.

These inspirational quotes can be powerful tools for providing comfort, motivation, and inspiration on the journey of forgiveness and healing. They remind us that forgiveness is not just about letting go of past hurts, but also about creating a brighter, more hopeful future for ourselves and for the world around us.

Journal Exercises:

❖ Choose one of the above quotes that resonates with you and write it down in your journal. Reflect on what this quote means to you and how it relates to your own journey of forgiveness and healing.

_____

_____

_____

_____

_____

_____

_____

_____

_____

_____

_____

_____

❖ Write down three situations or people in your life that you are struggling to forgive. Reflect on what is holding you back from forgiving them, and what steps you can take to move towards forgiveness.

_____

_____

_____

_____

_____

_____

_____

_____

_____

❖ Write down three things that you are grateful for in your life, even in the midst of pain or difficulty. Reflect on how gratitude can be a powerful tool for cultivating a more positive and hopeful mindset on the journey of forgiveness and healing.

_____

_____

_____

_____

_____

_____

_____

_____

_____

_____

Affirmations for self-compassion and self-love

Affirmations are a powerful tool for cultivating self-compassion and self-love. They are positive statements that help individuals to shift their focus away from negative thoughts and emotions, and towards more constructive and empowering ones. When used regularly, affirmations can help to build self-esteem, reduce stress and anxiety, and increase resilience. In the context of forgiveness and healing from emotional abuse, affirmations can be especially beneficial for counteracting self-blame and negative self-talk.

Here are some examples of affirmations for self-compassion and self-love:

❖ I am worthy of love and respect, just as I am.

❖ I forgive myself for any mistakes I have made, and I choose to learn from them.

❖ I am strong and resilient, and I can overcome any challenge that comes my way.

❖ I am deserving of happiness and joy, and I choose to focus on the positive in my life.

❖ I trust myself to make the right decisions for me, and I have faith in my own judgment.

❖ I choose to let go of past hurts and move forward with love and compassion.

❖ I am deserving of care and attention, and I prioritize my own needs and well-being.

❖ I am enough, just as I am, and I embrace my strengths and weaknesses with love and acceptance.

❖ I am capable of creating the life I want, and I take active steps towards my goals every day.

❖ I am deserving of forgiveness and compassion, both from others and from myself.

It can be helpful to repeat affirmations to oneself regularly, either silently or aloud. Some individuals find it helpful to incorporate affirmations into a daily self-care routine, such as repeating them during meditation, journaling, or exercise. Affirmations can also be written down and placed in visible locations, such as on a mirror or a computer desktop, as a visual reminder to practice self-compassion and self-love.

In addition to repeating affirmations, it is important to also take practical steps towards self-care and healing. This may include seeking therapy, practicing mindfulness and meditation, engaging in physical activity, and connecting with supportive friends and family members. By incorporating affirmations into a broader self-care routine, individuals can foster a sense of self-compassion and self-love that can support them through the process of forgiveness and healing from emotional abuse.

Overall, affirmations are a simple but powerful tool for cultivating self-compassion and self-love, and can be especially beneficial for individuals working towards forgiveness and healing from emotional abuse. By regularly affirming one's worth and value, individuals can begin to shift their mindset towards one of self-acceptance and self-love, which can support them in the journey towards forgiveness and healing.

Journal Exercises

❖ Write a letter to yourself as if you were your own best friend. Start with "Dear (your name)," and write down all the qualities you appreciate about yourself, the things you admire, and the ways in which you have grown. Use kind and encouraging language, and remind yourself of your worth.

_____

_____

_____

_____

_____

_____

_____

_____

_____

_____

_____

_____

_____

_____

_____

_____

_____

_____

_____

_____

_____

_____

❖ Reflect on a recent mistake or failure that you're struggling to forgive yourself for. Write down the mistake, how it made you feel, and any negative self-talk that you've been telling yourself. Then, challenge those thoughts by writing down three affirmations that counteract them. For example, if you're telling yourself "I'm such an idiot," write down affirmations like "I am smart and capable" or "I am deserving of love and respect."

_____

_____

_____

_____

_____

_____

_____

_____

_____

❖ Make a list of things that bring you joy and make you feel good about yourself. They can be big or small, and can include things like spending time with loved ones, listening to your favorite music, or accomplishing a goal. Refer back to this list when you're feeling down or need a reminder of the things that make you happy.

_____

_____

_____

_____

_____

_____

_____

_____

_____

_____

_____

❖ Practice gratitude by writing down three things you're grateful for each day. They can be anything from a good cup of coffee in the morning to a supportive friend or family member. Focusing on the good things in your life can help shift your perspective and increase feelings of self-compassion and self-love.

_____

_____

_____

_____

_____

_____

_____

_____

_____

❖ Write down a positive affirmation that resonates with you and repeat it to yourself throughout the day. You can write it on a sticky note and place it somewhere you'll see it frequently, like your mirror or computer screen. Some examples of positive affirmations include "I am worthy of love and respect," "I trust my intuition and make decisions that serve me," and "I am strong and capable of overcoming challenges."

_____

_____

_____

_____

_____

_____

_____

_____

_____

_____

In conclusion, forgiveness and healing are important aspects of our lives that we should actively pursue. It is not always easy, and sometimes we may feel lost or stuck, but with patience, effort, and the right tools, we can move forward towards a more positive and fulfilling life. Affirmations and inspirational quotes can be powerful tools in this process, reminding us to be kind to ourselves, to forgive others, and to let go of negative emotions. Remember, healing is not a destination but a journey, and it is important to be kind to ourselves and to seek support from those around us. With the help of these affirmations and quotes, we can continue on this journey with hope, positivity, and a deep sense of self-love and compassion.

CHAPTER 6: TOOLS FOR MOVING FORWARD

- ❖ Self-care practices for healing
- ❖ Building resilience and establishing healthy boundaries
- ❖ Steps for rebuilding trust and restoring relationships

Emotional abuse can leave lasting scars and trauma, making it difficult to move forward with confidence and trust in oneself and others. However, there are tools and practices that can help survivors of emotional abuse heal and regain their sense of self-worth and inner strength. This chapter will explore some essential tools and practices for moving forward after emotional abuse, including self-care practices, building resilience, establishing healthy boundaries, and steps for rebuilding trust and restoring relationships. By integrating these tools into your life, you can begin to move forward with greater confidence, inner peace, and a renewed sense of hope.

Self-care practices for healing

As a survivor of emotional abuse, I know firsthand how difficult it can be to prioritize self-care. For so long, I believed that taking care of myself was selfish or unnecessary. But over time, I learned that self-care is essential for healing and moving forward.

One powerful tool that has helped me on my journey is affirmations. Affirmations are statements that we repeat to ourselves to cultivate positive beliefs and behaviors. By using affirmations, we can shift our mindset and begin to view self-care as a necessary part of our healing process.

Here are some affirmations for self-care practices that have been helpful for me:

- ❖ I prioritize my physical, emotional, and mental health.

- ❖ I deserve to take care of myself.

- ❖ My needs are important and deserve to be met.

- ❖ I am worthy of rest and relaxation.

- ❖ I am allowed to say no to things that drain my energy.

- ❖ I am deserving of love and respect, especially from myself.

- ❖ I am capable of healing and moving forward.

- ❖ I am strong and resilient.

- ❖ I am deserving of happiness and joy.

- ❖ I am worthy of a life filled with abundance and positivity.

Incorporating affirmations into your self-care routine can be a powerful way to shift your mindset and prioritize your healing. Here are some journal prompts to help you incorporate these affirmations into your self-care routine:

❖ Which affirmation resonates with me the most? Why?

_____
_____
_____
_____
_____
_____
_____
_____
_____
_____

❖ How can I incorporate this affirmation into my daily routine?

_____
_____
_____
_____
_____
_____
_____
_____
_____
_____

❖ What self-care practices have I neglected in the past? How can I prioritize them now?

_____
_____
_____
_____
_____

_____

_____

_____

_____

_____

_____

❖ What obstacles have prevented me from prioritizing self-care in the past? How can I overcome them?

_____

_____

_____

_____

_____

_____

_____

_____

_____

❖ How can I show myself love and compassion today?

_____

_____

_____

_____

_____

_____

_____

_____

_____

Remember, self-care is not selfish. It is a necessary part of your healing process. By incorporating these affirmations into your self-care routine, you can begin to shift your mindset and prioritize your well-being.

Building resilience and establishing healthy boundaries

Building resilience and establishing healthy boundaries are crucial components of the healing process from emotional abuse. These practices enable individuals to develop the strength and skills necessary to protect themselves from further harm and overcome the negative effects of past abuse. In this chapter, we will explore the importance of building resilience and establishing healthy boundaries and provide practical strategies for doing so.

Resilience is the ability to adapt and recover from adverse situations. Building resilience requires developing coping strategies and a positive mindset, which can be challenging for individuals who have experienced emotional abuse. Emotional abuse can leave survivors feeling helpless, powerless, and with a distorted sense of self-worth. However, by actively working on building resilience, survivors can reframe their experiences and develop a sense of agency and control over their lives.

One way to build resilience is to practice self-compassion. This involves treating oneself with the same kindness, concern, and understanding that one would offer to a good friend. Self-compassion involves acknowledging one's pain and struggles without judgment or self-criticism. It involves accepting oneself as flawed but still deserving of love and compassion. By practicing self-compassion, survivors can develop a positive self-image and increase their capacity for resilience.

Another essential aspect of building resilience is developing healthy coping strategies. Coping strategies are the actions and behaviors individuals use to manage stress and anxiety. Effective coping strategies can help individuals regulate their emotions and maintain a sense of calm in challenging situations. Some healthy coping strategies include mindfulness, deep breathing, exercise, creative expression, and social support. By developing and practicing healthy coping strategies, individuals can increase their resilience and reduce the negative impact of emotional abuse on their lives.

Establishing healthy boundaries is another crucial component of the healing process from emotional abuse. Healthy boundaries involve setting limits on how others treat us and how much access they have to our personal lives. Survivors of emotional abuse often struggle with boundary-setting due to the manipulative and controlling behavior of their abusers. This can lead to a sense of powerlessness and a lack of control over one's life.

To establish healthy boundaries, survivors must first recognize and acknowledge the need for them. This involves understanding what behaviors and actions are acceptable and unacceptable in their relationships. Once survivors have identified their boundaries, they must communicate them clearly and assertively to others. This can be challenging for individuals who are used to minimizing their needs and feelings to avoid conflict. However, establishing healthy boundaries is essential for maintaining self-respect and protecting oneself from further harm.

In addition to setting boundaries, survivors must also learn to say "no" without feeling guilty or ashamed. Saying "no" is a healthy and necessary part of establishing boundaries and maintaining one's autonomy. Survivors must learn to prioritize their own needs and well-being and recognize that saying "no" is not a selfish act but a necessary one.

Finally, building resilience and establishing healthy boundaries require ongoing effort and practice. Survivors must be patient and gentle with themselves as they navigate the healing process. It may take time to develop healthy coping strategies and establish strong boundaries, but with persistence and dedication, it is possible.

In conclusion, building resilience and establishing healthy boundaries are essential components of the healing process from emotional abuse. By practicing self-compassion, developing healthy coping strategies, and setting and maintaining healthy boundaries, survivors can increase their resilience, protect themselves from further harm, and reclaim their sense of self-worth and agency. It takes time, effort, and patience, but the rewards of building resilience and establishing healthy boundaries are immeasurable.

Steps for rebuilding trust and restoring relationships

Rebuilding trust and restoring relationships after experiencing emotional abuse can be a challenging and lengthy process. It can take time to heal from the emotional wounds caused by the abuse and to learn how to trust others again. However, with dedication and effort, it is possible to rebuild relationships and establish trust once more.

Step 1: Recognize the Need for Rebuilding Trust

The first step towards rebuilding trust is acknowledging the need for it. In the aftermath of emotional abuse, it can be easy to feel like you never want to trust anyone again. However, isolation and mistrust can be damaging in the long term. It is important to recognize that the desire for connection and the ability to trust others is a fundamental human need.

Step 2: Take Responsibility for Your Part

In order to rebuild trust, it is important to take responsibility for your part in the relationship. This means being accountable for any actions or behaviors that may have contributed to the breakdown of trust. It may be difficult to do, but taking responsibility and apologizing for any harm caused can be a powerful step towards rebuilding trust.

Step 3: Communicate Openly and Honestly

Communication is key when it comes to rebuilding trust. It is important to communicate openly and honestly with the person you are trying to rebuild trust with. This means being transparent about your thoughts, feelings, and actions. It also means being willing to listen and validate the other person's feelings and concerns.

Step 4: Practice Patience

Rebuilding trust is not a quick process. It can take time to heal from the wounds caused by emotional abuse and to establish trust once again. It is important to be patient and not rush the process. It may be tempting to try to push the other person to trust you again, but this can be counterproductive. Trust needs to be earned through consistent actions over time.

Step 5: Set Boundaries

Establishing healthy boundaries is crucial when rebuilding trust. It is important to set clear boundaries around what behavior is acceptable and what is not. This may involve having difficult conversations and being willing to walk away from the relationship if necessary. Setting boundaries can help to establish a sense of safety and trust.

Step 6: Seek Support

Rebuilding trust can be a difficult and emotional process. It is important to seek support from friends, family, or a therapist. Having a support system can provide encouragement, guidance, and perspective. It can also help to work through any emotions that may arise during the process of rebuilding trust.

Step 7: Take Action

Ultimately, rebuilding trust requires taking action. This means following through on promises, being consistent in your behavior, and demonstrating your trustworthiness through your actions. It may take time to rebuild trust, but consistent and intentional actions can help to establish a foundation of trust and respect.

In conclusion, rebuilding trust and restoring relationships after emotional abuse is possible, but it requires effort, patience, and commitment. By recognizing the need for rebuilding trust, taking responsibility for your part, communicating openly and honestly, practicing patience, setting boundaries, seeking support, and taking action, it is possible to establish trust and connection once again. Remember, the process of rebuilding trust may be difficult, but the rewards of a healthy and trusting relationship are worth it.

In conclusion, healing from emotional abuse is a journey that requires time, patience, and effort. It is essential to prioritize self-care and establish healthy boundaries to prevent further harm. Building resilience is key to withstanding future challenges and setbacks. It is important to remember that forgiveness and rebuilding trust are also part of the healing process, but it is important to approach these steps with caution and only when both parties are willing and committed to making positive changes.

By practicing self-care, building resilience, and taking steps to restore trust and relationships, survivors of emotional abuse can reclaim their power and create a new, fulfilling life for themselves. It is important to remember that healing is not a linear process, and there will be ups and downs along the way. But with the right tools and support, it is possible to move forward and thrive. Always remember to be kind to yourself, celebrate your progress, and never give up on your healing journey.

CHAPTER 7 CONCLUSION

* ❖ Recap of the importance of forgiveness in healing from emotional abuse
* ❖ Encouragement for readers to embark on their own forgiveness journey
* ❖ Final words of hope and empowerment

Chapter 7 marks the conclusion of this emotional healing book, which has explored the critical role of forgiveness in healing from emotional abuse. Throughout the previous chapters, we have delved into the therapeutic benefits of sharing personal stories, the stages and practical exercises for fostering forgiveness, the common obstacles to forgiveness, and the tools for moving forward.

In this concluding chapter, we will recap the importance of forgiveness in the healing process and encourage readers to embark on their own forgiveness journey. We will also offer final words of hope and empowerment to those who may still be struggling with the effects of emotional abuse.

Recap of the importance of forgiveness in healing from emotional abuse

In this book, we have explored the powerful impact of forgiveness in the process of healing from emotional abuse. We have discussed how emotional abuse can have long-lasting effects on individuals, including low self-esteem, anxiety, and depression. We have also talked about how forgiveness is not about forgetting or condoning the abuser's behavior but rather about freeing oneself from the emotional burden and pain caused by the abuse.

We have covered several topics, including the definition of emotional abuse, the benefits of forgiveness, the stages of forgiveness, practical exercises for fostering forgiveness, common obstacles to forgiveness, and tools for moving forward. Throughout these chapters, we have emphasized the importance of self-compassion, self-care, and building resilience in the journey towards forgiveness and healing.

Forgiveness is a process that takes time and effort. It is not easy, but it is necessary for one's emotional well-being. Through forgiveness, individuals can break free from the cycle of pain and hurt caused by emotional abuse. Forgiveness allows individuals to let go of the anger, resentment, and bitterness that can consume them, and it enables them to move forward towards a brighter future.

The benefits of forgiveness are numerous. Forgiveness has been linked to lower levels of stress, anxiety, and depression, and improved physical health. Forgiveness also fosters healthier relationships and promotes inner peace and happiness. It is a powerful tool for personal growth and development.

Forgiveness is not a one-size-fits-all solution. The process of forgiveness looks different for everyone, and it may take longer for some than others. However, with patience, commitment, and the right tools and resources, forgiveness is achievable.

It is essential to remember that forgiveness is not about condoning the abuser's behavior or letting them off the hook.

It is about releasing oneself from the emotional burden caused by the abuse. Forgiveness is a gift that individuals give themselves, and it is not dependent on the actions of the abuser.

In conclusion, forgiveness is a vital component of healing from emotional abuse. It allows individuals to break free from the cycle of pain and hurt caused by abuse and move forward towards a brighter future. Through self-compassion, self-care, building resilience, and practical exercises for fostering forgiveness, individuals can take the necessary steps towards forgiveness and healing. Remember, forgiveness is not about forgetting or condoning the abuser's behavior, but rather about freeing oneself from the emotional burden caused by the abuse.

Encouragement for readers to embark on their own forgiveness journey

If you've made it this far, congratulations! You have taken the first step towards healing by reading and learning about the power of forgiveness. It takes courage to confront our pain and past hurts, and even more courage to begin the process of forgiving those who have hurt us.

The journey of forgiveness is not an easy one. It takes time, effort, and a willingness to face difficult emotions. But it is a journey that is well worth the effort. Forgiveness has the power to release us from the emotional prison of anger, resentment, and bitterness. It allows us to move forward and live a happier, more fulfilling life.

If you are ready to embark on your own forgiveness journey, here are some words of encouragement to keep in mind:

Be gentle with yourself: Forgiveness is not a one-time event. It is a process that requires time and patience. Be kind to yourself and give yourself permission to take things one step at a time.

Practice self-compassion: It's important to be compassionate towards yourself throughout the forgiveness process. Treat yourself with the same kindness and understanding that you would give to a friend.

Seek support: It can be helpful to have the support of friends, family, or a therapist as you navigate the forgiveness journey. Don't be afraid to reach out for help when you need it.

Set realistic expectations: Forgiveness does not necessarily mean reconciliation or a complete restoration of the relationship. Sometimes, forgiveness means simply letting go of the hurt and moving on.

Trust the process: Forgiveness is not always linear. There may be setbacks and difficult moments, but trust that the process will lead you towards healing and growth.

Remember, forgiveness is not a sign of weakness. It takes incredible strength and courage to forgive those who have hurt us. But the rewards of forgiveness are immense. By letting go of anger and resentment, we open ourselves up to greater love, joy, and peace.

So take a deep breath, and take that first step towards forgiveness. You are capable of healing, growth, and transformation. Trust yourself and trust the process, and know that you have the power to create a brighter future for yourself.

Journal Exercises :

❖ Reflect on a past hurtful experience. What emotions come up for you?

_____

_____

_____

_____

_____

_____

_____

_____

_____

_____

❖ How has this experience impacted your life?

_____

_____

_____

_____

_____

_____

_____

_____

_____

❖ Write about how you think forgiveness could potentially help you move forward.

_____

_____

_____

_____

_____

_____

_____

_____

_____

_____

_____

❖ Think about someone in your life who has hurt you. What specifically did they do that caused you pain?

_____

_____

_____

_____

_____

_____

_____

_____

_____

❖ Write a letter to them, expressing your hurt and your desire for forgiveness. You don't need to send the letter, but writing it can be a powerful exercise in releasing your emotions.

_____

_____

_____

_____

_____

_____

_____

_____

_____

_____

_____

❖ Write down five things you can do to practice self-care and self-compassion as you embark on your forgiveness journey. This could include things like taking time for yourself, practicing meditation or mindfulness, or seeking support from a therapist or trusted friend.

_____

_____

_____

_____

_____

_____

_____

_____

_____

❖ Consider any negative self-talk or limiting beliefs you may have about forgiveness. Write down these thoughts and then challenge them. Are they really true?

_____

_____

_____

_____

_____

_____

_____

_____

❖ How might changing your perspective on forgiveness help you move forward?

_____

_____

_____

_____

_____

_____

_____

_____

_____

_____

❖ Reflect on any past experiences where you have forgiven someone. What did this process look like for you?

_____

_____

_____

_____

_____

_____

_____

_____

_____

❖ What did you learn about yourself and your own capacity for forgiveness?

_____

_____

_____

_____

_____

_____

_____

_____

_____

_____

_____

❖ Use this reflection to inspire and encourage you on your current forgiveness journey.

_____

_____

_____

_____

_____

_____

_____

_____

_____

_____

Final words of hope and empowerment

As you come to the end of this book, I hope that you have gained valuable insights into the process of forgiveness and its importance in healing from emotional abuse. It is not an easy journey, but it is a necessary one. And it is a journey that you do not have to take alone.

Remember that forgiveness is a choice that you make for yourself, not for anyone else. It is a gift that you give to yourself, and it is a step towards reclaiming your power and finding peace. It is not about condoning or excusing the actions of your abuser, but about freeing yourself from the burden of resentment and anger.

As you embark on your forgiveness journey, here are some final words of hope and empowerment to guide you:

You are worthy of love and respect. No matter what you have been through, remember that you are valuable and deserving of happiness. Your past does not define you, and you have the power to create a better future for yourself.

Forgiveness is a process, not an event. It takes time, patience, and effort to heal from emotional abuse and forgive your abuser. It is okay to take it one step at a time and to seek support from others.

You are not alone. There are many resources available to you, including support groups, therapists, and hotlines. Don't hesitate to reach out for help if you need it.

Self-care is essential. Take care of yourself physically, emotionally, and spiritually. Practice self-compassion and self-love. Nurture your relationships with family and friends. Engage in activities that bring you joy and fulfillment.

Your journey is unique. There is no one "right" way to heal and forgive. Trust yourself and your instincts, and do what feels right for you.

Remember that forgiveness is a journey, not a destination. It is a process of growth and healing, and it requires patience, perseverance, and self-compassion. But it is also a journey that is worth taking. It is a journey towards freedom, peace, and empowerment.

As you move forward on your forgiveness journey, know that you have the strength and resilience to overcome any obstacles that may arise. You are capable of healing, of finding peace, and of living a life filled with joy and purpose.

Embrace the journey, and trust that you will emerge stronger and more whole than ever before.

In conclusion, I wish you all the best on your journey towards forgiveness and healing. May you find the courage, strength, and wisdom to forgive, to heal, and to live a life of joy and purpose.

Here are some resources that survivors of emotional abuse can use to continue their healing journey:

Therapy: One of the most effective ways to heal from emotional abuse is to work with a licensed therapist. A therapist can help survivors process their experiences, develop coping strategies, and work through any emotional trauma that may have resulted from the abuse. To find a therapist, survivors can ask for recommendations from their healthcare provider or use online directories such as Psychology Today or GoodTherapy.

Support Groups: Joining a support group can be a powerful way for survivors to connect with others who have had similar experiences. Many organizations, such as The National Domestic Violence Hotline, offer support groups for survivors of emotional abuse.

Self-Help Books: There are many excellent books that offer guidance and support to survivors of emotional abuse. Some popular titles include "The Body Keeps the Score" by Bessel van der Kolk, "The Courage to Heal" by Ellen Bass and Laura Davis, and "The Tao of Fully Feeling" by Pete Walker.

Hope, Healing, and Rising Strong Series: The Hope, Healing, and Rising Strong series by M.L.Ruscsak provides valuable insights and practical tools for healing from emotional trauma. The series includes "Finding Your Voice" "Surviving and Thriving," "Rising Strong," "Building a Better Future" and "Rising Above the Pain."

Meditation and Mindfulness Practices: Mindfulness and meditation practices can be powerful tools for healing from emotional abuse. These practices can help survivors become more aware of their thoughts and emotions, develop self-compassion, and cultivate a sense of calm and inner peace. Apps such as Calm and Headspace offer guided meditations and mindfulness exercises.

Exercise and Movement: Physical exercise can be a powerful tool for healing from emotional abuse. Exercise can help survivors release pent-up emotions, reduce stress, and boost their mood. Activities such as yoga, dance, and martial arts can also help survivors connect with their bodies and cultivate a sense of inner strength.

Creative Expression: Engaging in creative activities such as art, music, and writing can be a powerful way for survivors to express their emotions and connect with their inner selves. Creative expression can also help survivors tap into their intuition and develop a sense of empowerment.

Remember, healing from emotional abuse is a journey, and it is important to be patient and compassionate with yourself as you move forward. With the right tools and resources, it is possible to heal and thrive.

www.ingramcontent.com/pod-product-compliance
Lightning Source LLC
Chambersburg PA
CBHW051636120626
46551CB00014B/2109